Beginning Again:
Immigrating to America

by Elaine A. Kule

BEST PRACTICES IN READING
Classroom Library

Contents

What Is Immigration?

Imagine packing up everything you own and saying goodbye to relatives, friends, and neighbors. You get on a boat or airplane for a long trip. You arrive at a place where people look and sound different. The houses, stores, and schools are different. Even the air doesn't smell the same. It all feels so strange, but this is your new home now.

Each year, thousands of people all over the world leave their homelands. They **emigrate** to live in other countries. Most of these people come to the United States.

These newcomers, or **immigrants**, have many reasons for leaving their own countries. Some hope for better homes, better jobs, and better pay. Others want the freedoms Americans enjoy. They want to express their ideas and beliefs. They want to have more choices in their daily lives. Some immigrants hope to make America their permanent home. Others only live here for a short time.

Many immigrants move to America because they have found work here. Some come to attend American schools. When immigrants arrive, they often join relatives already living in the United States.

Immigrants sailed past the Statue of Liberty as they arrived in America.

People have been moving to the U.S. for hundreds of years. In the past, most immigrants came from Europe. Some came to America so they could worship and vote the way they wanted. Many immigrants now come to earn a better living. Most newcomers are from Mexico, India, and China.

Moving to a new place can be difficult. Immigrants often settle in areas where other people from their home country are already living. This helps make the adjustment a little easier. The new immigrants can keep their **native** language and traditions while adjusting to different surroundings. In time, they adjust, or **adapt**, to their new home.

The United States has laws that control the **immigration** process. Many people want to move to the United States. But, not all of them are allowed to come and stay. The U.S. Citizenship and Immigration Service (USCIS) decides how long each immigrant may stay. The USCIS also handles the process immigrants must go through to become American **citizens**. This process is called **naturalization** (nah-cher-al-ih-ZAY-shun).

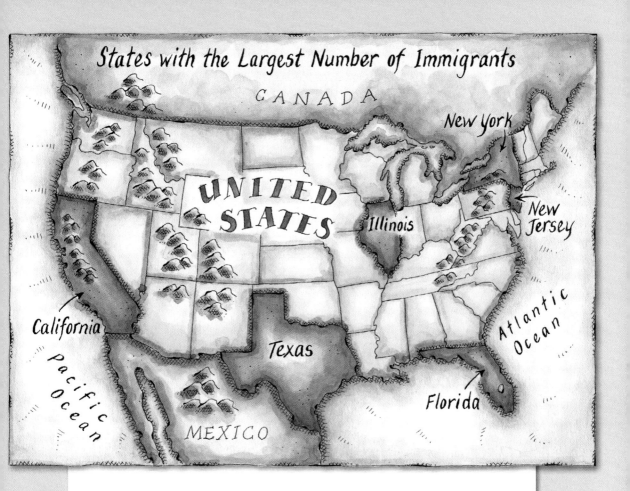

States with the Largest Number of Immigrants

The largest number of immigrants have settled in California, New York, and Florida. Other states with many immigrants are Texas, New Jersey, and Illinois.

Immigrants in the U.S. can have jobs and own houses. They can go to school anywhere in America. However, they can't vote in any elections unless they become official citizens.

Many immigrant children are happy about moving to the United States. They may also be sad to leave their home countries. There will be many changes when they move here. Some may have to learn to speak English. Others will have to adjust to living in large cities. They will need to learn new customs. All of them will have to begin their lives again in a new country.

Jocelyn

Mohammed

The children interviewed in this book have all immigrated to the United States. Read on to discover how they have begun new lives in America.

Anna

Tom

1 Why have people continued to come to America for so many years?

2 What is an immigrant?

3 Why is adjusting to life in a new country sometimes difficult?

4 If you could live in another country, which country would it be? Explain your answer.

From Mexico: Jocelyn

I was born in Mexico and grew up speaking Spanish. Because Mexico's **population** is growing, jobs are harder to find there. Many people from my country leave to find work in the United States. My father found a job in New York City. My mother, my two sisters, and I moved here to join him.

My aunt, uncle, and cousins live near us in the same apartment building. I like having everyone close together. In Mexico, we had a house and a backyard. Here in New York City, we go to Central Park. That's like a backyard—a huge backyard!

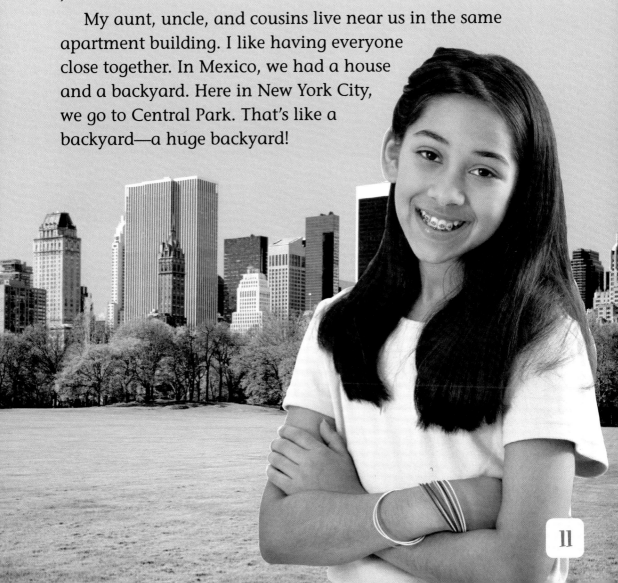

We live in a neighborhood where most people speak Spanish. I'm in a **bilingual** (bye-LING-wuhl) class in school. My teacher speaks both Spanish and English. That makes learning easier. Getting to school is also easier here than in Mexico. I used to have to take a long bus ride.

When I'm not wearing my school uniform, I dress in pants and T-shirts or sweaters. In Mexico, I wore mostly shorts and blouses. The weather is a lot warmer there. Mexican summers are long and hot. The winters are cooler, and the weather is nice most of the time.

I like how the seasons change in New York. Before I came to America, I'd never worn gloves or a coat! I remember seeing snow for the first time here. I watched it for hours. I loved how pretty it made everything look.

Central Park is pretty in the wintertime.

I'm learning many things in school.

Learning English was hard. During my first year in America, a teacher's helper had to sit with me. She translated what the teacher said into Spanish so I could understand.

I got through that year because there wasn't a lot of reading or writing. First grade was harder, though. Learning to read was difficult. I practiced a lot. I got better at it, but it took a while. Now reading is one of my favorite things to do. I also am better at speaking English. At home, though, I still speak only Spanish with my family.

I enjoy listening to both Mexican and American music. After I finish my homework, I play the radio. I do that a lot when I'm cleaning the room I share with my sisters. They say I'm too neat, but I say they're too messy! We also watch TV when there's time. I think American television helped me learn English.

My cousins love playing soccer!

When the weather is nice, my cousins and I go outside to jump rope or play soccer. Soccer is a big sport in Mexico. If there's an empty field, you'll always find people playing soccer! Mexico has professional soccer teams. There are also lots of teams of people who play just for fun.

I love pizza and french fries, but my favorite food is a *tostada* (to-STAH-duh). That's a tortilla (tor-TEE-yuh) that's fried until it becomes crisp. I eat it with just lettuce and cheese on top. Some people also add meat, onions, and beans.

I have the same chores here that I had in Mexico. I help my mother with laundry, washing dishes, and taking care of my little sister.

We enjoy many of the same holidays here as we did in Mexico. But in Mexico, we don't have Halloween. We don't go trick-or-treating for candy. Instead, we celebrate the Day of the Dead. It usually falls between late October and early November. It's around the same time as Halloween, but it's a different kind of holiday. In Mexico, this is a time to remember people in our family who have died. We go to the cemetery and visit their graves. Some people call it the Mexican Halloween, but it's not like an American Halloween at all.

In America, Thanksgiving is a big holiday. Everyone has turkey, so my family has it, too. We celebrate this holiday because we're thankful. We're healthy, we have food and a home, and we have each other.

We honor loved ones on the Day of the Dead.

The holiday I like most is Christmas. My family and I celebrate it the same way in America as we did in Mexico. We spend weeks getting ready. We decorate our apartment, go shopping for food, and we buy presents. On Christmas Day, we have a big dinner with our relatives. Everybody exchanges gifts. Then we take pictures, sing, dance, listen to music, and just have fun. We also telephone our family in Mexico. It's the best time of the year for me.

The Christmas tree in Rockefeller Plaza

I talk to my grandmother who still lives in Mexico.

I'm very happy in America, but I miss my family back in Mexico. I especially miss my grandmother. Talking to her on the telephone when I can is great, but it's not enough.

My parents say that we may move back to Mexico someday. They miss our family, too. If we move back, I'll be happy. But, I'll also be very sad. I like living in Mexico *and* the United States. I've had wonderful teachers here. I've also made a lot of really good friends. I feel like America has welcomed me.

1. What has helped Jocelyn adapt to life in America?

2. Why was school hard for Jocelyn when she first got here?

3. Why does Jocelyn like living in America?

4. What special ways do you and your family celebrate holidays?

From China: Tom

It takes fifteen hours to travel by airplane from China to San Francisco, California. Tom made this long trip alone to live with his grandparents.

Adjusting to life in America has been almost easy for him. Living with relatives who know about the city has been very helpful. Also, San Francisco has many Asian residents. Read what Tom told a reporter from his school newspaper about his immigration to America.

REPORTER: Hi, Tom. I'd like to ask you about moving to America from China.

TOM: Hi. What would you like to know?

REPORTER: How long have you been in America?

TOM: Three months.

REPORTER: Why did you come to the United States?

TOM: I came to the United States to go to school. My parents think I'll get a better education here. They couldn't move here because they own a shop in China. That's why I'm living with my grandparents.

REPORTER: How did you get ready for living in America?

TOM: My mother sent me to classes to learn English.

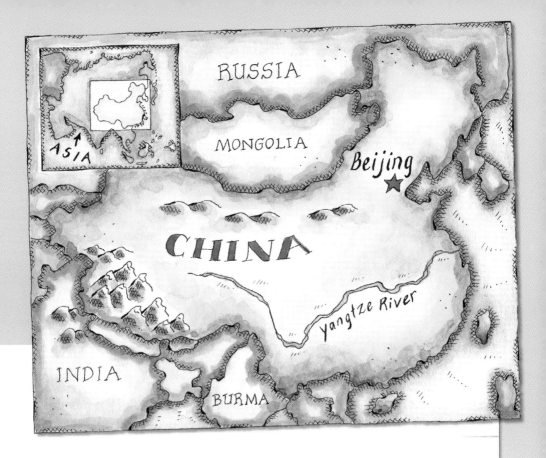

REPORTER: Was English hard or easy for you to learn?

TOM: It was hard. I'm still learning it!

REPORTER: What was the most difficult thing about leaving China?

TOM: I had to leave my friends and family behind. I really miss my parents and my sister back in China.

REPORTER: Do you think they'll come to live in the United States?

TOM: I don't know. I hope so!

REPORTER: What activities do you do in the U.S. that you didn't do in your country?

TOM: In China, I never did arts and crafts or played group games like basketball or baseball.

REPORTER: Do you dress the same here as you did in China?

TOM: Not really. I wear a lot more clothes here. The weather in San Francisco is a lot cooler than in China.

REPORTER: What American foods do you like most?

TOM: Hamburgers, french fries, and ice cream!

REPORTER: Are there any foods from China that you miss?

TOM: No. The food here tastes much better to me. But my grandmother still cooks Chinese food like they have at home.

REPORTER: What sports do you play in the U.S.?

TOM: I play basketball at school. I also play handball at a club in the city. They have a good weekend program for kids to play sports.

REPORTER: What Chinese customs or traditions do you still follow?

TOM: I speak Chinese with my family. We celebrate the Chinese New Year with some other relatives who also live here. It's always in January or February. Our New Year's Day falls on a different date each year. We have a big meal on New Year's Eve. Then we exchange gifts and try to stay up all night.

REPORTER: Do you enjoy living in America?

TOM: Yes. I've made a lot of friends and I'm learning new things at school. People have been nice to me. And, the cable cars are fun!

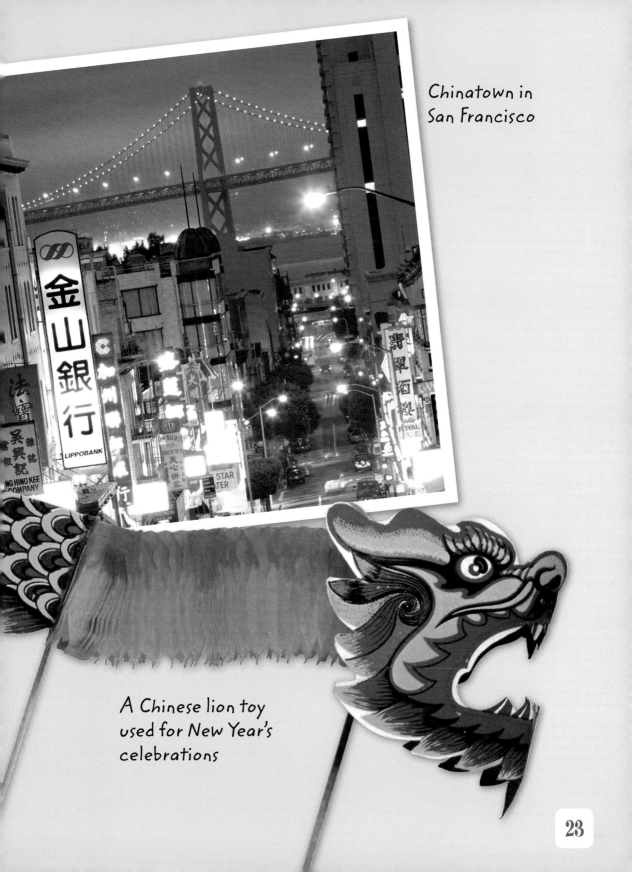

Chinatown in
San Francisco

A Chinese lion toy
used for New Year's
celebrations

1 Compare and contrast Tom's life in the United States and in China.

2 Why did Tom come to America?

3 Why does Tom continue some customs from China in his new life in America?

4 What could you do to make a student from another country feel more at home in America? Explain your answer.

From the Republic of Georgia: Anna

Anna is a talented tennis player. She grew up in the Republic of Georgia. This country is located in southwestern Asia, between Turkey and Russia. Anna moved to Florida to attend a tennis training center. Here's what she said about living in America.

I've been playing tennis for many years. America has the best training programs, so it made sense to move here. Still, it was difficult to leave Georgia. My parents didn't have enough money to bring the whole family here. So, my father and I came to Florida. My mother and sister stayed home.

RUSSIA

ASIA

Black Sea

GEORGIA

DAGESTAN

Caucasus
Mountains

Tblisi

TURKEY

I love to
climb the hills
in Georgia.

It wasn't easy leaving the only country I'd ever known. I also felt sad about saying goodbye to my grandparents and other relatives. I wasn't sure when I'd see them again.

Another thing that worried me was the language. When I got here, I only spoke Georgian. Also, our alphabet is completely different from the English alphabet. How could I do well in school if I didn't understand what anyone was saying or writing?

When I arrived in Florida, I thought it was beautiful. I saw palm trees for the first time. The weather here is so warm! It's perfect for playing tennis. The only thing I don't like are those horrible hurricanes!

I took English classes to learn the language. I was glad that I wasn't the only student at the training center who was from another country. There are lots of kids from other nations here. I've made some good friends and that has helped me get used to living in America.

Palm trees are everywhere in Florida!

I was really busy the first year, but I still missed my mother and sister a lot. I also missed Georgian food, especially the bread. Georgian bread is baked in big clay ovens.

During my second year here, my mother and sister came to join us. Like most Georgian families, we're very close. I was so happy when they arrived. Having my whole family here made America seem more like home. We even celebrated Thanksgiving, with turkey and everything!

Maybe the ovens make this bread so delicious.

One thing I never did back home was swim. I learned how when I got to Florida. I couldn't wait to take my first swim in the Atlantic Ocean. It's still one of my favorite things to do.

The training center I attend wants students to do more than just play tennis. Our teachers make sure we get to do other sports like horseback riding, biking, canoeing, and even bowling! We also go to concerts, movies, plays, and museums.

I play a lot of tournaments in Florida. Most of the time my family goes with me. It's a great chance for us to travel, and I'm glad we can do it together.

In Georgia, students can leave school after the tenth grade. But I want to continue my education in America. I enjoy learning. It's not really hard for me to play tennis and attend classes.

I can honestly say that I enjoy living here. Americans are very friendly. Now that my whole family is here, I like living in America a lot. I think it would be hard to leave now. I want to go back to Georgia to visit, of course, but I hope to make the U.S. my country someday.

1. What helped Anna become more comfortable living in America?

2. Why did Anna immigrate to the United States?

3. Why does the training academy want their students to do more than play tennis?

4. Would you move to another country to practice a sport? Why or why not?

From Guinea, West Africa: Mohammed

Mohammed came to America from the Republic of Guinea (GIH-nee) in West Africa. Guinea has mountains, forests, and sandy beaches. The weather is usually hot and humid. Except in the north, heavy rains fall from April until November.

Mohammed has lived in New York City with his father and brother for three years. Here's his story.

REPORTER: Why did you come to America?

MOHAMMED: For a better education. My parents didn't have a chance to go to school when they were young. They wanted me to get a good education and maybe go to college.

REPORTER: How did you feel about coming to America?

MOHAMMED: I was excited, and sad. I was excited because you see things in the movies about America. You think, wow, I want to live in a place like that. In Guinea, I lived in a small village. I have 15 brothers and sisters. All my friends and family came to the airport to wave goodbye. That was sad. I was also afraid because I didn't know if they'd let me into America.

REPORTER: What do you mean?

MOHAMMED: I came over here by myself. My father and brother were already here. When I got off the plane, I had to go through immigration. My heart was beating really fast. Back home, people said if you made it past the immigration booth, everything was okay. They'd let you in. The man was really nice, though. I got in with no problem.

REPORTER: What was your first week in America like?

MOHAMMED: It was strange. Everything looked so different! The buildings were really tall. And even though my father and brother were here, I felt really lonely. I didn't have any friends. I would see kids playing basketball with their friends and it would make me sad. I was homesick a lot. It was also hard because I didn't speak the language.